Nostradamus
and the
Attack on New York

By Chris Conrad

Creative Xpressions • California
www.chrisconrad.com

Dedication

This book is dedicated to all victims of global terrorism and violence, particularly those who died in the attacks on New York and Washington DC on September 11, 2001.

A special dedication is offered to those who died in the Pennsylvania air crash in a valiant effort to stop a second terrorist attack against Washington DC. May their heroism be long remembered.

Let freedom ring.

Nostradamus and the Attack on New York

By Chris Conrad.
Editorial assistant: Brynn Boyle. Research assistant: Cherice Green.
ISBN 0-9639754-6-3

Based on the original French predictions of Michel de Nostredame (1503-1566), simply known as Nostradamus.

Acknowledgements:

We wish to acknowledge the AP, Reuters, ABC, NBC, CBS, CNN, Newsweek and all the news media, dictionaries, encyclopediae, atlases and history books upon whose reports we relied in making these connections Also, we reviewed numerous transcriptions, translations and interpretations for this book. While we did not use any single version to compile these translations, we would particularly like to acknowledge the contributions of two insightful books that were most helpful in this analysis:

Roberts, Henry C. *The Complete Prophesies of Nostradamus*. American Book-Stratford Press, Inc. New York NY. 1949. This was the first complete English language translation of Nostradamus' original writings. This scholarly work has served as the basis for many later translations.

Cheetham, Erika. *The Prophesies of Nostradamus*. Perigee Books / G.P. Putnam's Sons. New York NY. 1973. This is a thorough study of the quatrains, with a good translation that is informative and easy to read.

If you want to see the complete verses, we recommend either of these.

Published by Creative Xpressions, El Cerrito CA.
Printed and bound in the USA by Central Plains Printing.
First edition release date: November 15, 2001. 96 pages, black and white.
Perfect bound. Laminated cover. List price: $9.95.

To order books and other products from our catalog, contact:
PO Box 1716, El Cerrito, CA 94530 USA • 510-215-8326
Email: Mikki@hr95.org

Visit the Chris Conrad / Creative Xpressions web page:
www.chrisconrad.com

Disclaimer: Michel Nostradamus died in 1566 AD. His work is subject to many different interpretations. We have tried to provide an accurate transcription and literal translation of his verses. We used popular solutions to several of his anagrams rather than concoct our own. This is but one possible interpretation of his words. The reader may well find other possibilities hidden within.

We leave the final interpretation to you.

— *The Author*

Nostradamus and the Attack on New York

Introduction: Prediction or Coincidence? **9**
Quatrain I:1, I:2, VI:100

1. The attack and surrounding imagery **13**
Quatrain II:29, VI:34, VI:97, II:46, X:49, I:87, X:72, IX:92, II:30

2. Close but no banana **33**
Quatrain IX:73, X:74

3. The background: Successful predictions? **37**
Quatrain II:19, I:50, IX:51, IX:65, I:63, VIII:70, II:89, I:91, I:41, III:60

4. Hints at who may have done what **59**
Quatrain VI:100, VI:78, II:79, II:9, VIII:20

5. Beginning of the end? **69**
Quatrain II:22, I:55, IV:43, VIII:77, I:62

6. Better things to come? **83**
Quatrain III:27, V:41, VI:24, IX:66

Index 95

Introduction

Nostradamus — Predictions or coincidence?

Michel Nostradamus was a French physician and prognosticator born on December 14, 1503, who wrote predictions in verses of four-lines each, called quatrains. He successfully predicted the deaths of two French kings during his lifetime, Henri II in verse I:35 and Francis II in X:39. He predicted the rise of Henri IV to the throne over his two older brothers.

When these and several others of his predictions came to pass, Nostradamus had to revise his verses to obscure certain details, using symbols and anagrams to hide the specific identities of groups and individuals he described. He used metaphor and cryptic historical references to disguise his predictions. He deliberately scrambled the sequence of his verses so they were out of chronological order, although one finds occasional sets of two or more consecutive verses that seem closely related. Much of this was done to avoid political pressure and persecution by the Justices of Paris. So the quatrains come to us as riddles.

This book began with the events of September 11, 2001 when we saw the televised image of a fireball in the sky over New York City. The Twin Towers of the World Trade Center, a signature of the New York skyline, were exploding in flames. Many people were reminded of ominous images from Nostradamus: *"A conflagration approaches the great New City ... a huge scattered flame leaps up..."* (VI:97) and *"in the sky will be seen a running fire, dragging long sparks."* (II:46) The towers burned for a matter of minutes, then crumbled to the ground. Some of us decided to look at those predictions again. Within his images are eerie, detailed similarities to those of the commercial news media.

This raised the question, are these coincidences or predictions? At the time of Nostradamus' death in 1566, the Americas had only recently been discovered and remained largely unsettled. Science and medicine were struggling to come out from under the Inquisition. Petty intrigues ruled the courts of Europe, and it could take months to travel from one country to another. Yet he provided detailed glimpses of a distant future; of popes, European kings and emperors. A mighty new nation would rise in the West. By the 20th century, global powers would emerge and World Wars rage. Later, people would travel safely by air, but calamity comes with the new millennium: an aerial fireball would send tremors through the great New City. During the Cold War, that image was said to predict a nuclear attack on New York. A new interpretation has now been thrust upon us.

Yet his vivid imagery still holds up. Nostradamus claimed visions of tomorrow and a voice to describe it. He sat in a dark room with a wand and a tripod to conjure up pictures of the future, then he painted them with his poetry.

He describes his method of divination:

> I:1 — Sitting alone at night in secret study; it rests on the brass tripod. A slender flame comes out of the emptiness and makes one utter that which should not be believed in vain.
>
> I:2 — The wand in the hand is placed in the middle of the tripod's branches. With water he sprinkles both the hem of his garment and his foot. A voice, fear; trembling through his sleeves. Divine splendor; the divine sits nearby.

One more comment from Nostradamus: Don't knock his predictions unless you can do better. In his words:

> VI:100 — Those who read this verse think upon it maturely: the profane, vulgar and ignorant should not be attracted. All astrologers, idiots and barbarians stay away, he who does otherwise, let him be a priest to the rite.

Nostradamus has been credited with accurate predictions for almost five centuries. Hence this book. It is a selection of his work showing the quatrains where we found the most vivid similarities to the attack on New York.

These lines are transcribed from handwritten notes that are about 450 years old. We tried to stay as true as possible to his original words. To avoid fake verses and corrupted translations, as are often found on the Internet, we used books that were at least 20 years old. Our research took three separate transcriptions of Nostradamus' verses, studied different translations, then reconciled them against a French dictionary to finalize the language. Since Nostradamus wrote in verse, we tried to follow the poet's original phrase sequence, as well. We include the original French for your personal comparison and interpretation.

As a final note, we did not base our interpretation on astrology, numerology or revised dates. We used his stated astronomical alignments and the dates as he wrote them. This is important to know, because the calendar has repeatedly been adjusted since Nostradamus' day, while he used his own dating system cross referenced with astronomical phenomena. Not all the verses have language in them that establishes a time frame. Some of these quatrains we offer are general enough to apply to numerous circumstances and interpretations, but others are very specific in visual or empirical detail. Where we found metaphoric similarities, we noted them for purposes of comparison, but did not assert them as fact. What we found most interesting were the verbal descriptions he wrote compared to news reports of the day. We don't ask you to believe: just to be objective.

Since this book is being written in the midst of epic events, we foresee a need for future editions. Stay tuned.

— *Chris Conrad*

Chapter 1

The attack on New York

Many people are looking for a way to release the stress and trauma caused by the news and repeated broadcast of pictures showing the devastation of a major metropolitan center. Over and again the same footage was repeated to turn a common set of images into cultural icons. It left many people speechless and gave them nightmares. The Pentagon was hit too; but it was the scene of the Big Apple with a gaping, smoldering wound that absorbed the news media and the nation's attention. Who saw that one coming?

If someone asked you to write a four-line poem describing the attack on New York, what would you say? That's essentially what Nostradamus did when he wrote his predictions. He gazed into his tripod to visualize an event, then gave himself four lines per stanza to describe it. He made sets of one hundred verses, referred to as a *Century*, then numbered them sequentially. Not all have survived.

For the sake of clarity, the notation shorthand we use is to list the Century by Roman numeral and verse by Arabic number. For example, I:1 refers to Century one verse one, and VI:34 is Century six verse 34.

Think of Nostradamus' quatrains as poems that anyone might have written about that day, mixing narrative with metaphor and visual imagery. That's how we approach his words here; as settings, events and here and there a metaphor or poetic figure of speech. We tried to remain as empirical as possible. You can compare this translation with others to look for more subtle possibilities.

Read the verse and our analysis, then judge for yourself how accurate his words and descriptions are.

Marwan al Shehhi
Suspected pilot

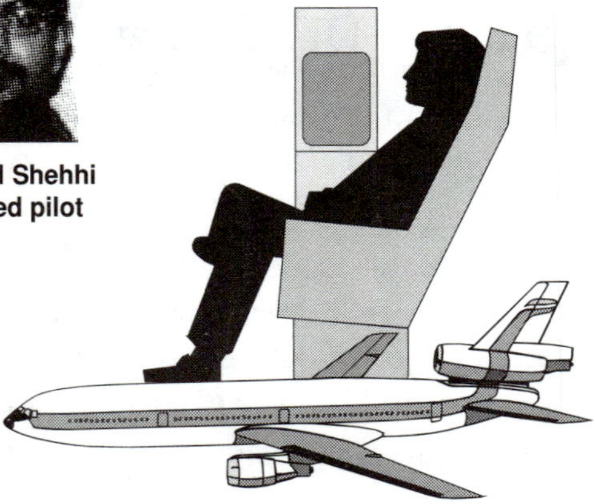

Mohamed Atta
Suspected pilot

II:29

L'oriental sortira de son siege,
Passer les monts Apennins, voir la Gaule:
Transpercera le ciel les eaux & neige
Et un chacun frappera de sa gaule.

The man from the East will come out of his seat,
Over the Apennine mountains to see France:
He will cross through the sky, the waters & snow
And he will strike everyone with his rod.

Hani Hanjour
Suspected pilot

Ziad Jarrah
Suspected pilot

THE TERRORIST GOT OUT OF HIS SEAT — Because of its reference to air travel, this quatrain seems to relate to the present age and merits our consideration.

In the first line a *man from the East comes out of his seat*. Poetically, that language could represent his political homeland, regime or stronghold. But what if it was meant literally? These words could apply to a terrorist passenger who gets up out of his seat on the plane. In his hand is a ceramic knife that had passed unnoticed through the airport security. This describes what happened on four domestic airliners on September 11, 2001. Bands of hijackers commandeered American Airlines flights 11 and 77, and United flights 175 and 93. They took over the controls. The consequences were terrible and tragic.

Line two depicts a man traveling to *France* over the *Apennine Mountains*, in Italy. This is the general direction that the terrorist hijackers traveled on their way from North Africa and the Middle East to New York City, as seen on the map on the facing page. Did suspected mastermindOsama bin Laden or other members in his violent Al Qaeda organization travel this specific route at some time? Bin Laden was born in Saudi Arabia, lived in Sudan and then with the Taliban in Afghanistan. Line three seems very modern as the man flies *across skies, waters and snow* in his travels.

In the last line the man lashes out and *strikes with his rod*. That could reflect corporal punishment, such as the Taliban's caning or stoning people who violate any nuance of their fundamentalist version of Islamic law. The airliners themselves are somewhat rod shaped, with wings attached. If the rod is a metaphor of an unwarranted and violent attack on humanity, that works, as well.

This first quatrain of the series contains fairly accurate details in each line, with even deeper implications for those inclined to read between the lines.

VI:34

De feu volant la machination,
Viendra troubler au grand chef assiegez:
Dedans sera telle sedition,
Qu'en desespoir seront les profligez.

The machine of flying fire,
Will come to trouble a great, besieged chief:
Within will be such sedition,
That those abandoned will be in despair.

BESIEGED BY JETS AND FLAMES — Although people still traveled by foot, horse or carriage in his day, here Nostradamus practically coins the phrase *"flying machine."* The word *fire* in line one may mean flame, as in the combustion within a jet engine, or it could mean a blazing conflagration, as in the explosion that followed the collision.

As the second line states, the aircraft hijacked and used to attack New York and set the World Trade Center on fire certainly did cause *trouble* for President and Commander in *Chief* GW Bush. He was *besieged* by the Chinese capture of a US spy plane soon after taking office in a legally disputed election, at the appointment of the US Supreme Court. His party lost control of the Senate within a few months of his taking office. The patriotic surge that swept the nation after the attack gave his popularity rating a boost, but also created a global and economic crisis for him to manage.

The third line may reflect the kamikaze pilots having been trained in aviation within the USA. They did board the planes without raising suspicion and strike from within; or perhaps by *sedition* Nostradamus hints at something even more sinister. Did insiders help the hijackers bring weapons onto the plane, or were they given financial and logistical support by people within the USA? We will have to see what evidence is uncovered over time.

The final line paints a bleak picture of people trapped in the New York rubble, unable to be rescued and regretfully *abandoned* to die. With the explosion, the crush of the buildings' collapse, clouds of asbestos-tainted dust, blood and agony, then rainstorms that turned the dust to sludge: *despair* is not too strong a word.

He hits it on every line in this verse, with line three being the most ambiguous. Nostradamus' words show a sincere compassion for the victims of the attack.

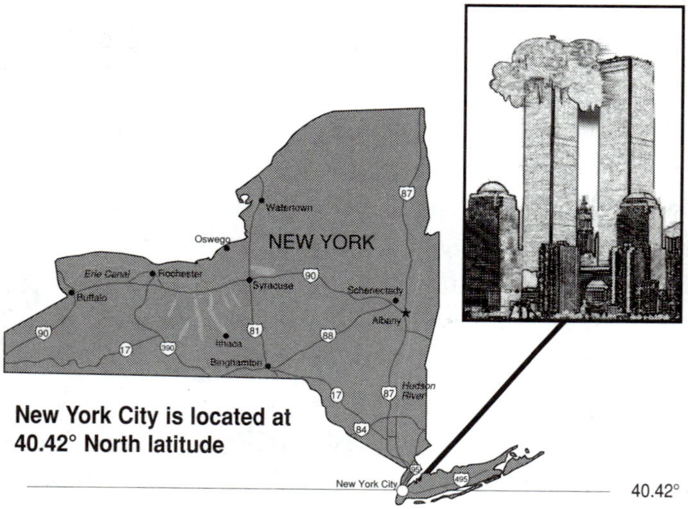

VI:97

Cinq & quarante degrez ciel bruslera,
Feu approcher de la grand cite neuve,
Instant grand flamme esparse sautera,
Quand on voudra des Normans faire preuve.

At 5 & 40 degrees the sky will burn,
Fire approaches the great New City.
Instantly a huge, scattered flame leaps up,
When they want to have proof of the Normans.

FIREBALL OVER THE NEW CITY — New York City lies at approximately 40.5 degrees North latitude. Otherwise this opening scene could not have been articulated much more clearly if Nostradamus had been watching the color TV footage and writing down what he saw there.

On September 11, 2001, two hijacked airliners *approached* the New York city skyline with jet engines blazing and tanks filled with jet fuel. They accelerated into the World Trade Center twin towers and exploded. *Instantly a huge scattered flame leapt up,* as described in line three: a fireball over the city. The conflagration spread. A cloud of smoke and debris billowed over the streets of the great American city. The inner cores melted and the buildings collapsed.

Nostradamus description works well in the first part of this stanza, despite a minor confusion about the location of downtown New York: *45 degrees* aligns with Salem, OR, Minneapolis, MN, and Montreal and Ottawa in Canada.

The last line gets obscure with the *Normans*. What has France got to do with it? Does he echo the call for a "Normandy Invasion" against terrorism? Does it correlate to the August, 2001 arrest of Zacarias Moussaoui, the Moroccan man who held a French passport when he entered flight school — but wanted only to learn how to maneuver an airliner in midair, not to take off or land? The FBI claimed that he was one of the intended hijacker-pilots.

Perhaps it's a tongue-in-cheek reference to himself, Nostradamus being French and his name beginning with the letters *No*. That would mean the attack would be seen as *proof of Nostradamus*. It is intriguing, but subsequent events may shed more light into his enigmatic remark.

For this overall verse we give line one partial credit for being close, but dock it a little for weird language on the latitude or being off by a few degrees. Lines two and three are dead on. The last line is in the "wait and see" category.

II:46

Apres grâd troche humain plus grand s'appreste,
Le grand moteur les siecles renouvelle,
Pluye, sang, laict, famine, feu & peste:
Au ciel veu feu, courant longue estincelle.

After great misery for mankind,
even greater approaches,
When the great cycle of centuries is renewed.
It will rain blood, milk, famine, war & disease:
In the sky will be seen a running fire,
dragging long sparks.

BURNING WALLS CRUMBLE FROM THE SKY — There were important technological and social advances in the Twentieth Century, but there also was plenty of *misery*, with World Wars, regional wars, disease and starvation.

In his first line, Nostradamus warns that worse times may lie ahead. The *cycle of the centuries* — ten of which equal one millennium — began over, as described in the second line, in the year 2001. That's also when the World Trade Center was hit in New York City.

The third line is a grotesquely vivid depiction of the carnage, mixing human *blood* with *milk* from the restaurants and vending machines that were located in the upper floors of the buildings. Then broader consequences are described, but *famine, war and disease* are always happening somewhere on earth. The Afghanis had been living in drought and hunger for years, and during the attacks, food was dropped to stem hunger in the border camps. War was declared by the USA soon after the attack, and by early October began allied strikes against the Taliban with massive aerial attacks. Then a wave of anthrax was seeded around the USA by mail to the news media, the US Congress and elsewhere.

Of all the visual depictions, this last line is one of the most impressive. Television reports of the World Trade Center were relentless in the days after the attack, and filled with video loops combining images of the towers blown up first in a tremendous fireball and then crashing down in a crush of debris and *sparks*. The term *courant* literally refers to running like the current of a stream, here composed of smoke and ash flowing from the sky. Visually, it did look like the walls came *running from the sky* crumbling and smoldering, as the towers accordioned floor by floor and collapsed straight down into the ground.

Unfortunately, everything in this quatrain works; even the last part of line three.

X:49

Jardin du monde aupres de cité neufue,
Dans le chemin des montagnes cavées,
Sera saisi & plongé dans la cuve,
Beuvant par force eaux soulphre envenimées.

The world garden near the new city,
In the road of the hollow mountains,
It will be seized & plunged into the tank,
Being forced to drink water poisoned with sulfur.

CALLING NAMES — The descriptive names Nostradamus gives in this verse come so close that it's eerie.

It was the World Trade Center, not the *World Garden*; but he got part of the name right. It could connect to the Biblical tower of Babel and the Hanging Gardens of Babylon, as he mentions in II:30; or maybe it relates to nearby New Jersey — the Garden State. There was no such thing as a global economy, an international trade center or even a skyscraper during the Renaissance, when he wrote. He almost got New York City right, too, but left out the *York*. Not bad, for a *new city* that hadn't yet been settled and wouldn't plant its first hemp until some 50 years after his death.

The *road of the hollow mountains* of line two works as a poetic description of that city's maze of highways and silhouette of skyscrapers, in which the attack occurred. New York City is a hub of global transportation and commerce. The structures of the high-rise office towers loom tall, like mountains; but the buildings themselves are hollow, consisting of rooms into which people and furnishings are placed.

Two aircraft were *seized* and set on target. Two 110-story towers were engorged in flames and *plunged* to the ground. The WTC basements and subterranean infrastructure did form a basin, but not a *tank* in the literal sense of being used for liquids or gas. The modern expression that someone *tanked* means they fell down or hit bottom.

The other unexplained element here is the line about being forced to drink *poisoned water*. The FBI repeatedly warned about this as a terrorist threat. There was a *sulfur* spill of a train in Northern California on September 11, 2001, but it seems an unlikely link — the water supply was not affected. Maybe it's an alchemic reference or a symbol.

On this quatrain, Nostradamus did pretty well in a blubbering sort of way. It's like he has the right words, just not articulated very clearly.

I:87

Ennosigee, feu du centre de terre,*
Fera trembler autour de Cite neufue:
Deux grands rochers long temps feront la guerre,
Puis Arethusa rougira nouveau Fleuve.

Earthshaking,* fire from the center of the earth,
Will cause tremors around the New City:
Two great rocks for a long time will war,
Then Arethusa will redden a new river.

* Greek. *Ennosigaeus* was a title for Neptune, meaning Earthshaking

EARTHSHAKING FIRE, TWO ROCKS — This looks like a Nostradamus-near miss at first, but on closer evaluation it holds up as a fairly accurate depiction.

The second line makes it pretty clear he's talking about New York again, but the *earthshaking fire from the center of the earth* implies an underground explosion or a volcanic eruption. But this conflagration was fed by jet fuel — refined from petroleum oil pumped from the bowels of the Earth. Granted, it's not the true *center* of the Earth, but it does come from miles underground. And remember that poor old Nostradamus was describing the images he divined with a rod. So, if someone like him saw oil being pumped from miles underground, he might reasonably characterize it as being from the center of the earth. The collapse of the Twin Towers was *earthshaking* and it caused *tremors around the city*. If there's a volcano in New York City, though, that would fulfill this verse even better, but it's still pretty good.

The image of the *two rocks* in the quatrain's third line evokes the famous stony pillars of the World Trade Center towers in the New York skyline. However, in this case it says *for a long time they will war*, so it seems Nostradamus meant it as a metaphor for two nations, cultures or religions: the rock of Christianity (St. Peter's name meant *rock*) and, by extension, the rock of Islam. As a metaphor, it has open possibilities. However, Osama bin Laden has since called for a holy war, so we're leaning towards that interpretation. President GW Bush said that this war will take years. Given the spiraling crises and calls for revenge in media and government, that sounds like a real danger.

It is curious that the letters "USA" are found in the last line's mystery character *Areth-USA*. This lends itself to the implication that a long war involving the USA will *redden a river* with blood. This verse is a mixed call on the tragedy, or more, depending on what happens next.

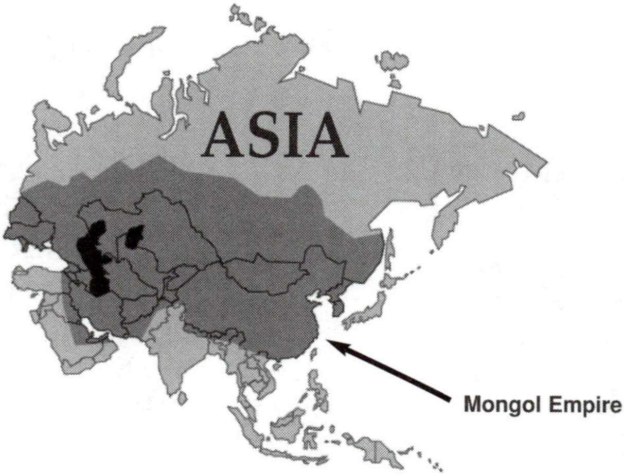

X:72

L'an mil neuf cens nonante neuf sept mois,
Du ciel viendra un grand Roy d'effrayeur.
*Resusciter le grand Roy d'Angolmois,**
Avant apres, Mars regner par bon heur.

In the year 1999 and seven months,
From the sky will come the great King of terror.
To revive the great king of the Angolmois,
Before after, Mars reigns through the early hour.

* *Angolmois* is considered an anagram for Mongols

KING OF TERROR, RETURN OF THE MONGOLS — Because the second line of this verse is so striking, with terror being directed from the sky, it is easy to forgive the little problem in the first line.

There are two years and two months difference between the date Nostradamus gives (*July, 1999*) and the September 2001 attack on New York. After 450 years, to miss by 26 months does not seem so bad. Plus, there have been several revisions to the calendar since then, and Nostradamus had his own system of calculation using the celestial bodies. Another curiousity is that the term *mois* can translate as a month or as a month's *wage,* in which case this could indicate a form of payback for earlier actions.

Line two is a gem: *From the sky will come the great King of terror.* No need to say more.

Angolmois, in line three has been interpreted that this King who brings terror from the sky is trying to *revive the Mongol* empire. The 13th Century Mongols controlled a broad swath from the Middle East across Asia all the way to China's Pacific coast, broken into four states or Khanates. The Central Asian Khanate included the Tarim Basin, Dzungaria, eastern West Turkestan, and Eastern Afghanistan. The Persian Khanate included Persia (Iran), Mesopotamia (Iraq), western West Turkestan, and western Afghanistan. They include the countries from where Osama bin Laden allegedly orchestrated the attack. Does this imply that there is a plan afoot for world domination, or at least Asia? This is likely true at any given moment of human history.

Mars, mentioned in the last line, was the Roman god of war, so the implication is that wars will rage around this time of day. The first plane hit the World Trade Center at 9:03 am EST, an *early hour* throughout the USA. It was the morning on the East Coast, break of day in California and in Hawai'i people woke up to news of the attack.

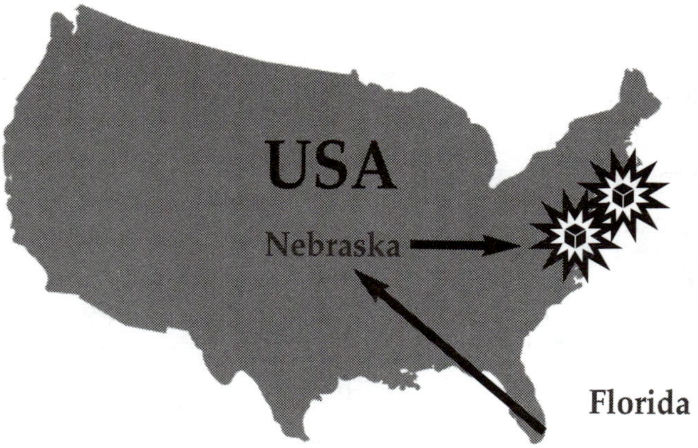

Bush's route in relation to the two attacks

IX:92

Le Roy voudra dans cité neufue entrer,
Par ennemis expugner l'on viendra,
Captif libere faulx dire & perpetrer;
Roy dehors estre, loin d'ennemis tiendra.

The king will want to enter the new city,
Through its enemies they come to subdue it,
A captive freed falsely to speak & act;
The king outside,
he will keep far from the enemy.

New cafeteria hit at the Pentagon, Washington DC

WASHINGTON DC, ESCAPE OF PRESIDENT BUSH — This verse is subject to at least two interpretations. If the *king* in the first line refers to the mastermind of the terrorist attack, the first two lines are a description of his strategy to enter *the new city* and *subdue* it using our own domestic commercial aircraft flown by enemy pilots.

Alternatively, perhaps line one's king depicts GW Bush, who upon hearing of the attack may have wanted to get back to New York or Washington DC, where the Pentagon was in flames. In either case, the second line would seem to refer to the terrorists who attacked.

There were many hostages taken *captive* on board the aircraft, as mentioned in the third line, but none were *freed, falsely* or otherwise. A more interesting fulfillment could be the people who were arrested after the attack and then released. Perhaps they were released with the intention to watch where they go, what they say, and what they do in order to collect further evidence. Or it could mean that someone may be set free who was not really innocent.

The fourth line offers two interpretations, as well. *The king* could apply to GW Bush, who was *outside* the city when Washington DC was attacked. His security came into play to protect him within moments of the attack, and he was *kept far away,* shuttled from his public relations event in Florida to a Nebraska bunker before being allowed to return to the Capitol when it had been secured. The alternative interpretation would be that the person who masterminded the attack did so from afar and will elude, or at least attempt to elude, capture by the USA and its allies.

Overall, not a very compelling quatrain, except for its relation to Bush's itinerary. The main problem with this prediction is its lack of specific details on which to hang an interpretation.

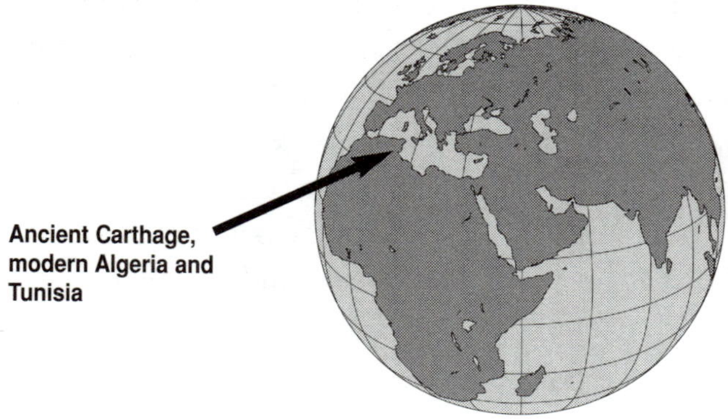

II:30

Un qui les dieux d'Annibal infernaux,
Fera renaistre, effrayeur des humains:
Oncq plus d'horreur, ne plus dire journaux,
Qu'advint viendra par Babel aux Romains.

A man who the infernal gods of Hannibal,
Will revive the terror of humanity.
Never before more horror,
nor the journals tell of worse,
Than will happen through Babel to the Romans.

* *Babel* was an ancient city located in modern Iraq

NEWSPAPERS CALL ATTACK WORST EVER — Ancient Carthage controlled an area that now includes Tunisia and Algeria in North Africa. *Hannibal* was a general who came from Carthage to attack the Roman Empire in 118 BC.

Hannibal became famous for bringing elephants from Africa over the mountains and attacking Italy from the North. The Romans were terrified by the burly beasts and fled in disarray. The first time, that is. They quickly learned how to chase the elephants right back onto Hannibal's own men, however, and Rome ultimately won the Punic wars. Line one makes an oblique reference to the general and his era that preceded Muslim culture. It seems to suggest that someone from an Arabic region is not a true Muslim. Nonetheless, he becomes a very dangerous figure.

Line two mentions *terror of humanity* again, whereas *terrorism* is a contemporary way of describing such acts of aggression. It's this line and phrasing that make one want to connect the quatrain with the attack on New York.

Most Americans will agree with line three that this was the worst single instance of terrorism yet to occur on the US mainland. Certainly no greater *horror* has occurred here in our lifetime, at least not in one day. Curious is his use of the term *journals,* because there were no daily newspapers at the time of his writing. Nostradamus seems again to have coined the term, so the translation sounds very modern.

The last line indicates that the *Romans,* European forces, will suffer a catastrophe through Babel, a reference to the Biblical Middle East. The city of *Babel* was known for its tall towers and the Hanging Gardens of Babylon. It is said to be where human speech separated into different languages.

Overall, this is not a great match. The ancient metaphor of lines one and four are too obscure to readily apply to the known facts. But line two works nicely, and line three is pulled straight out of the headlines.

Chapter 2

Close but no banana

People have been interpreting the prognostication of the astronomer Nostradamus for a long time. Sometimes they find amazing similarities, sometimes they torture the words to force their own preconceptions into the poetry.

Worse yet are those who either fabricate verses in Nostradamus' name, or combine lines from various verses in order to put together one verse that is very precise in its description of events. You can come up with some good stuff that way, but it's cheating. As we now know, the seer deliberately wrote vague and cryptic references into his work to keep people guessing. In the preceding verses, we kept our interpretation to the simplest manner possible, and found some amazing correlations. There were also some inconsistencies and misfires.

Just because a certain quatrain doesn't work very well doesn't mean that people will not cite it, and this chapter makes that case for your consideration.

Here we present the two verses that get most of the unwarranted attention, one because it gives the legendary description of a the king who wears a Blue Turban, the other because it refers to the new millennium, ostensibly the Year 2001.

We find both of these to be unsatisfactory, but here they are anyway, along with a brief explanation of their strengths and shortcomings.

IX:73

Dans Fois entrez Roy ceiulee Turban,
Et regnera moins evolu Saturne,
Roy Turban blanc Bizance cœur ban,
Sol, Mars, Mercure prés la hurne.

Into Foix enters a king with a blue turban,
And will reign for less than a revolution of Saturn;
King with the white turban, proclaims the heart of Byzantium,
Sun, Mars, Mercury near the horn (Aquarius).

THE BLUE TURBAN — This is the famous *king in a blue turban* quatrain that people talk about. The planetary alignment described in line four occurred on February 18, 1981.

The king with a blue turban enters a city in southern France. That resembles Allatoyah Khomeini's rise from a revolutionary in France to overthrow the Shah of Iran in 1979 and put hard line clerics into power, launching a new wave of militant Islamic fundamentalism. But he wore a black turban, not blue, and was not in France in 1981.

Another king has a *white* turban. Turkey is the modern country most closely associated geographically with Byzantium. It is currently a secular state. The Taliban wear white turbans, as mentioned, or sometimes black turbans; but they are based in Afghanistan.

The revolution of Saturn lasts 29.5 years, but the reign of the blue turban is shorter. Adding it up comes to August 2010. We'll see what happens by then.

X:74

Au revolu du grand nombre septiesme,
Apparoistra au temps jeux d'Hecatombe,
Non esloigné du grand eage milliesme,
Que les entrez sortiront de leur tombe.

The cycle of the great seventh number completed,
It will appear at the time of the games of mass graves,
Not far from the great age of the millennium,
That the buried will come out of their graves.

THE NEW MILLENNIUM — This seems like a possible date around the *millennium* year 2001, as stated in the third line of this quatrain. Or maybe not.

Some assert that the cryptic reference to the *great seventh* refers to the year 7000, with a Biblically inspired description of the Second Coming of Christ. Maybe, but it also begs the question of how the dead are to *come out of their grave.* The prognosticator's words could describe the recent unearthing of ancient mummies and graves, or perhaps the opening of mass graves in the Balkans to identify victims of the genocide of the former Yugoslavia.

The City of New York gave urns of ash from the World Trade Center rubble to the families of those who died in the attack, to honor the victims and the memory of their lives. Other than being set at the millennium, we don't find any strong corollary to the historical events of the attack.

Chapter 3

The background: Successful predictions?

Nostradamus did his writing not long after Columbus came to the New World. Yet, as seen above, he wrote of a new city of skyscrapers that would one day be stricken from the air.

Was this due to a special power or ability, or just a lucky guess? It would be easy to write off these visions of the soothseer if they were not part of a broader pattern. This depiction was not an isolated vision to Nostradamus, who predicted nearly a thousand specific incidents that set a context for one another. Gazing into his tripod and flame, he challenged us to find patterns and secrets in his timeline.

This next chapter will show some of the close approximations he described to actual events and historical personages other than the attack on New York. He provided his readers with plenty of surrounding information to give a good description of the circumstances useful to keep the attack in perspective.

Some of these examples may relate to other incidents and individuals as well as the ones we point out here. People have found allusions to Hitler and Napoleon, the French Revolution, the British empire, etc. Looking is fun, but we only discuss a handful of his quatrains here.

As Nostradamus paints each scene for us, we try to see through his eyes as we look at our own world. The pictures are dim, but provocative. Who was that person? What was that date? What stories will we find hidden there?

II:19

Nouveaux venus, lieu basty sans deffence
Occuper place par lors inhabitable,
Prez, maisons, champs, villes prendre à plaisance,
Faim, peste, guerre, arpen long labourable.

Newcomers will build a place without defenses
To occupy a place then inhabitable,
Meadows, houses, fields, towns
taken with pleasure,
Famine, plague, war, extensive arable land.

SETTLEMENT OF AMERICA — Although America was just a nebulous coastline in Nostradamus' day, and the USA did not yet exist, his depiction of the Manifest Destiny conquest of the New World is quite detailed.

The *newcomers* of line one describes European colonists against whose weapons, diseases and numbers the indigenous peoples had *no defense*. He seems to recognize that the USA would one day have the largest unfortified national border in the world. North and South, it borders friendly nations: Canada and Mexico. East and West are oceans that discourage foreign invasion. Despite its large military forces in America and the rest of the world, or perhaps because of them, most of its inhabitants had felt safe from attack. However, after the attack on New York new interest arose in airport and border security.

The second line is interesting. The land was *inhabitable* when Europeans arrived here, but through pollution and development the environment has been seriously degraded. Nostradamus seems to imply that eventually the land or parts of it may become uninhabitable.

Meadows are naturally occurring, but most of the native American tribes were nomadic so, with a few exceptions, they did not have houses or towns in the sense that we do today. The *meadows, houses, fields* and *towns* of line three would be those developed by the settlers readily after they took the land to enjoy for their own use.

The last line links *famine, plague* and *war* — three tools used to decimate the native population — with the expansion of farmland. In a very real way, this was how the native peoples would be cleared from the land in the USA in the 19th century: 300 years after Nostradamus wrote this verse.

The nation of Israel might also meet this description, but since the Jewish settlers were theoretically returning to an ancestral homeland, they do not quite seem to be *newcomers*.

I:50

De l'aquatique triplicite naistra,
D'un qui fera le Jeudy pour sa feste.
Son bruit, loz, regne, sa puissance croistra,
Par terre & mer, aux Oriens tempeste.

From the three aquatics he will be born,
One who will make Thursday his holiday.
His renown, praise,
rule and power will grow,
By land & sea, bringing trouble to the East.

PRESIDENT OF THE USA — Nostradamus here mentions the *three aquatics* — Cancer, Scorpio and Pisces of the Zodiac. Their respective terms are June 21 to July 21, October 21 to November 21 and February 21 to March 21. They include the Fourth of July (founding of America), first Tuesday in November (election day) and March 20 (original inauguration day for the President, later changed to January 20).

Otherwise, the aquatics of line one, which pertains to water, could correlate to three oceans that border the USA: Atlantic, Pacific and Arctic (see map, page 38). Since people aren't born with three sun signs, the *birth* of one who makes *Thursday his holiday*, from line two, seems a metaphor of the creation of the office of the President of the United States. The USA is a world power that clearly identifies itself with Thursday as a national holiday — nothing is more distinctively American than Thanksgiving Dinner.

On the facing page are icons of three of our most beloved presidents, George Washington, Abraham Lincoln and John F. Kennedy. By the end of the 20th Century, the USA was often referred to as the Earth's only remaining superpower and the policeman of the world. As stated in line three, the long line of US presidents has earned global *renown, praise, rule and power*.

For more than two centuries, those attributes have grown on both *land and sea,* as described in the fourth line. America's history of *bringing trouble to the East* is legion, from Japan to Korea, China to Vietnam, Iraq to Iran and now Afghanistan. With the attack on New York, a new round of troubles began, and the attack on Afghanistan brought trouble to the East once again. Unfortunately, these problems also have a tendency to come home to roost.

Nostradamus really got everything right this time around. It's a bit over generalized, but "Thursday" was a nice clue, and the broad scope of his prediction fits the topic.

IX:51

Contre les rouges sectes se banderont,
Feu, eau, fer, corde par paix se minera,
Au point mourir ceux qui machineront,
Fors un que monde sur tout ruynera.

Against the red ones sects will unite,
Fire, water, iron,
the rope through peace will be destroyed,
At the point of dying are those who plot,
Except one who above all will ruin the world.

PROTESTANTISM & INDUSTRIAL AGE — The first line of this quatrain seems disjointed from the rest. Nostradamus states that different *sects* will unite against *the red ones*, which usually means Catholic cardinals. This may refer to the growing influence and power of Christian Protestants and the decline of the Church, or alternatively, the churches uniting against the atheistic "Reds" of Russia.

The next line is analogous to the industrial revolution of the 19th and 20th centuries. *Fire* for energy, *water* for irrigation, and *iron* for industry. The *rope* historically was made with hemp. During the time of the industrial revolution, the hemp industries became weaker as its basic products were replaced with non-renewable resources. Timber replaced hemp in paper and building supplies. Fossil fuels replaced hemp sails to power ships, transportation and industry (windmills). Steel cables, then nylon, replaced hemp ropes. Cotton became the main textile fabric. Then came the federal US ban on hemp under the name *marijuana*. During World War II the ban was suspended, but during the relatively peaceful half-century that followed, war was declared on hemp and billions of dollars spent to suppress the crop which was once required to be grown right here in the USA. Today there is a federal death penalty on growing hemp. Thus was *the rope* destroyed during a time of peace.

The closing two lines may depict near-fatal environmental destruction that overcomes the planet as a result of industrial pollution and deforestation. Those who cause the pollution fall victim to their own schemes. In the end, however, the main culprit who *ruins the world* manages to escape. Perhaps this reflects the ability of the wealthy to avoid the consequences of their ecological crimes, while the negative effects and costs are borne by the rest of society.

Applied to the attack on New York, these last two lines describe the suicide attacks of the conspirators, while the mastermind behind the plot survived the carnage.

IX:65

Dedans le coing de Luna viendra rendre,
Où sera prins & mis en terre estrange,
Les fruicts immeurs seront à grand esclandre,
Grand vitupere, à l'un grande loüange.

He will come to take himself
to the corner of the Moon,
Where he will be taken & placed on strange land.
The unripe fruit will be of great scandal,
Great blame, to the one shall be great praise.

MOON LANDING — The first two lines give a literal description of the 1968 lunar landing, with a man being taken and placed on the moon's soil. This one is pretty hard to dispute, except to note that the moon does not have a *corner*, so who knows what that means.

Nostradamus' description of the moonscape as a *strange land* is vague but accurate. Remember that as recently as the 19th century the moon was said to be made of green cheese, so at least he debunked that myth. What makes this one so special is that the time of moon explorations was very brief. Well into the 20th Century people doubted that it would ever be achieved. After great fanfare man walked on the moon, but after a few years the program stopped. People could reach the moon, but it turned out they had not found much use for it. Maybe we just weren't ready yet, as the *unripe fruit* of line three implies.

Lines three and four are impossible to pinpoint because they're too general. One way to relate it to the first line is to look at the major participants in the space race, the USA and Russia. The unripe fruit may represent totalitarian socialism and democratic capitalism. To the Taliban and other Muslim fundamentalists, both comprise a *great scandal*. The USA represented idolatry and decadence, while the Soviets were godless secularism. The Taliban first used military aid provided by the USA to drive Russian forces out of Afghanistan then, predictably, turned against the USA.

By the end of the century, one of these ideologies, Russian state communism, was widely disgraced to the global community. State communism was given *blame* for many of the world's ills. The other, western capitalism as embodied by the USA, was given *great praise* and emulated. This works as a metaphor that makes the first two lines even more compelling.

I:63

Les fleaux passees diminue le monde,
Long-temps la paix, terres inhabitees:
Seur marchera par le ciel, terre, mer & Onde:*
Puis de nouveau les guerres suscitees.

Pestilences being past,
the world becomes smaller,
For a long time peace, lands inhabited:
Safe they will march through the sky, land,
sea & Wave:
Then again the wars will start up.

* Also refers to financial *transactions* and *dealings*

LATE 20th CENTURY — This is a beautifully lyrical depiction of the late 20th century.

It was an age of great medical advances, such as inoculations and antibiotics to control the *pestilence* and plagues of smallpox and polio. Cancer and AIDS were still unconquered, but as Nostradamus said in the first line, many diseases had been controlled or eliminated. Who knew at the beginning of the century that, before it ended, a trip to Europe from California would take less than a day? The telecommunications and transportation revolutions led to rapid globalization that seemed to shrink the world. The phrase "It's a *small world*" was popularized as a song title.

This was also the era of the so-called Pax-Americana extending from the end of World War II when the USA assumed a role of global power and dominance. Wars did rage, but they did not always involve the USA. Most were generally characterized as "contained," regional incidents involving rogue states while the bulk of the world was at peace, as described in line two. Europe enjoyed its longest era of peace since the Roman Empire.

Nevertheless, line three correctly and incredibly talks of transcontinental air travel in the same casual tones that we use in modern society. Then comes the clincher: *Safe they will march through the sky*. Not only did Nostradamus predict air travel, but even the safety of using airlines! Certainly, one thing that was destroyed by the events of September 11, 2001 was our sense of safe travel. Then there is this last little tidbit, the word *Wave*, capitalized. This indicates this is not just a wave of water, the implication being radio waves. Hence this could reflect that people would conduct financial transactions through the airwaves: banking by satellite.

A few days after the attack on New York, Congress declared war, as Nostradamus clearly states in the last line of this poem. He seems to envision more than one conflict ahead. Looks like another four for four.

The area of ancient Mesopotamia is located in modern Iraq by the Tigris and Euphrates rivers.

VIII:70

Il entrera vilain, meschant, infame
Tyrannisant la Mesopotamie
Tous amis faict d'adulterine dame,
Terre horrible noir de phisonomie.

The villain will enter, wicked, infamous,
Tyrannizing Mesopotamia.
All friends made by the adulterous lady,
The land horrible and black of aspect.

SADDAM & THE 1991 GULF WAR — The first line is an unflattering portrait of Iraqi leader Saddam Hussein. *Wicked villain* is a reasonably accurate image, at least as he has been portrayed by the majority of Western commercial media. He is a man of *infamous* reputation.

This opening description could relate to a lot of historical villains, however, until you get to the second line, which places him in a specific geographic region. His rule over his homeland of Iraq, known as *Mesopotamia* in antiquity, could be called *tyrannical*. The Kurds who live under him certainly regard it as such, and have been waging a long guerrilla counterinsurgency against him for decades, with erratic support from the USA.

Line three appears to be a metaphor that Nostradamus borrowed from the *Bible*. Babylon is another ancient civilization that existed in the area of modern Iraq. The whore of Babylon is an *adulterous lady* who seduces mankind before the Apocalypse, the final war between good and evil (Revelation chapters 18-19). She is also described as being a wealthy city that is destroyed by fire in one hour, and all the world watches the smoke rise from her ruins. This religious prophecy is a very rich and complex symbol that we leave to the reader to explore on his or her own.

As a contrast, the last line seems like it was taken from news reports written in 1991. When the USA's incendiary bombs rained down on Iraq, oil wells burned for months on end. Even worse, oily rain spread throughout the region when petroleum-laden smoke was caught in rain. Huge areas of *land* were *blackened*. Such was the *horrible* environmental destruction caused by the Gulf War.

So this quatrain matched the Gulf War literally in lines one, two and four. The implication of line three depends on how much significance you give to the recurrent references to Babylon that occur throughout these selected verses.

II:89

Un jour seront amis les deux grands maistres
Leur grand pouvoir se verra augmenté:
La terre neufue sera en ses hauts estres,
Au sanguinaire, le nombre racompté.

One day will be friends the two great leaders;
Their great power will be increased:
The new land will be at the height of its power,
To the man of blood, the number is reported.

THE 1990s TO SEPTEMBER 2001 — By virtue of some other quatrains I did not include, Nostradamus predicted that in the late 20th century there would be *two great leaders* that became adversaries. This led many people in the 1980s and 90s to interpret his tale of a fiery air attack on New York as being a Soviet nuclear missile.

This verse seemed to contradict that interpretation, and presents a more accurate picture of subsequent events. The Soviets and USA entered into a *friendly* relationship in the late 1980s, when Gorbachev dismantled the USSR and ended the Cold War. Things continued to be relatively friendly throughout the 1990s, so the first line is accurate. If you substitute the UK or a different great leader for Russia, that works as well, since the USA has many allies.

As far as the second line is concerned, the USA did grow in *power* in the 1990s. In most senses of the word, however, Europe and Russia's power and influence seemed to wane as the USA economy overshadowed them.

The third line looks good, though. The USA hit *the height of its power*, with massive global reach and influence. It dominated the world militarily and economically. There was a sense of invincibility that has been tarnished in an abrupt and reprehensible way. People felt suddenly vulnerable, seeing the "Big Apple" of America's eye with a smoldering wound where, until one fateful day, stood a global economic powerhouse: the World Trade Center. Two mountainous buildings, 110 floors tall, held thousands of men and women in offices, shops and restaurants. Cell phone-toting executives made deals that would make or break fortunes.

On September 11, 2001, some 5,000 people were inside the towers, when four airliners took off into the morning sun. Among their passengers were 19 terrorists, on a mission of death, destruction and revenge.

Then, *to the man of blood*, the number was reported.

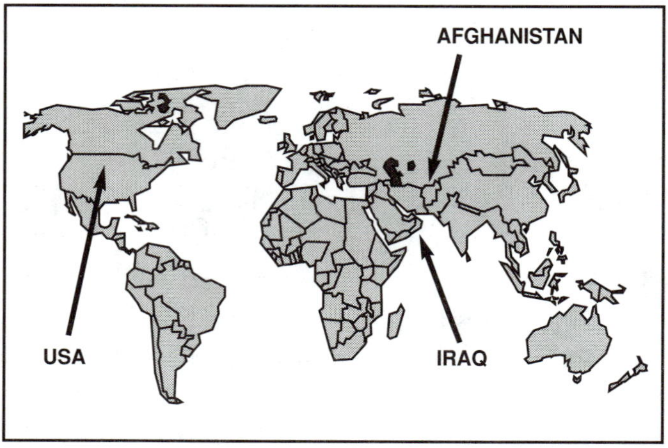

I:91

Les Dieux feront aux humains apparence,
Ce qu'il seront autheurs de grand conflit.
Avant ciel veu serain, espee & lance,
Que vers main gauche sera plus grand afflict.

The Gods will make it appear to humanity,
That they are the authors of a great war.
Before the sky seen as serene, weapon & lance,
That against the left hand
will be greater damage inflicted.

STAR WARS DEFENSE & ABM TREATY — Whatever the real motive of the attack on New York, Nostradamus warns that at least some people will *make it appear* that this is a war inspired by religion. Certainly to hear bin Laden and the television evangelists spouting their venom, one would think that this is a holy war and a new Crusade if not the Apocalypse. If Muslim terrorists were involved, as it appears, the odds are very good that they felt they were warriors and martyrs in a *jihad*, or holy war. However, Nostradamus' words of lines one and two casts doubt upon that argument, indicating that the gods are not *authors of a great war* at all: someone is making it appear that way.

Line three pitches an interesting angle. Shortly before the attack on New York, President Bush announced that his administration would unilaterally rescind the Anti-ballistic Missile (ABM) Treaty and that the US would increase its investment in the SDI, space-based defense initiative, also known as Star Wars. The effect of these two actions would result in breaking treaties and using the serenity of space as a launching platform for both defensive and offensive *weapons*. With the attack on New York, civilian aircraft were also used as weapons, so this is another hit for the Seer.

Finally, consider that on contemporary maps the West (and therefore the USA) is on the left hand side. (See facing page.) The fourth line indicates that the USA will sustain the *greatest damage*. If this had been associated with an attack by a communist state, the *left* might have a very different implication. However there are indications elsewhere that the West will ultimately prevail, though at devastating cost.

Some modern interpretations use the word "rockets" or "missiles" to translate the French, *lance*, because a lance is a weapon flung at an enemy, as is a missile. Does this refer to the USA lobbing missiles at Afghanistan?

I leave that to you to decide.

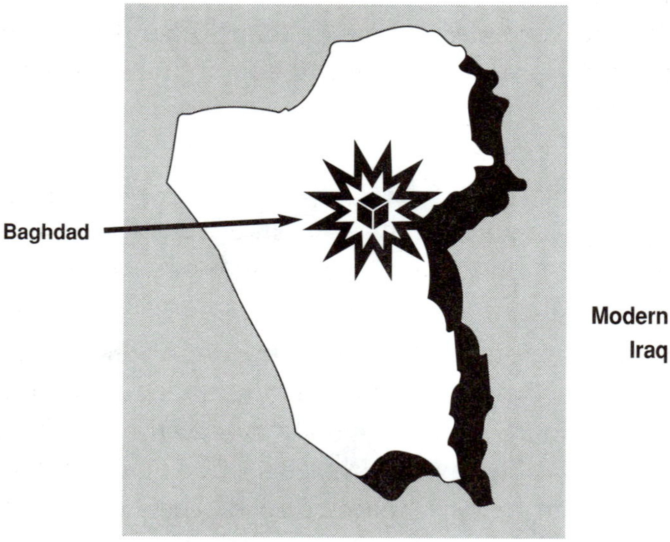

I:41

Siege en Cite & de nuict assaillie;
Peu eschapes non loing de mer conflict,
Femme de joye, retours fils defaillie,
Poison & lettre cache dedans le plic.

The city is besieged & by night assaulted;
Few escaped, not far from the sea a battle,
A woman faints with joy at the return of her son,
Poison & letters hidden within the folds.

BOMBING OF BAGHDAD — Baghdad, Iraq was assaulted by night in January 1991, while millions of people watched on CNN, as Nostradamus described in the first line of this stanza. The Allies *assaulted the city by night*. The attack left the sky ablaze with flames as the USA and its allies pounded the Iraqi capital for days on end. Its economic infrastructure was pulverized, water and power lines cut, bridges bombed out regularly, Iraq's capitol destroyed.

Casualties on the ground were very high. A defining moment of the elder President Bush's Gulf War was its infamous "Turkey Shoot:" a strip of highway along which retreating Iraqi troops had to flee back from the Coast of Kuwait, and *few escaped*. Having wiped out Iraq's air force, Allied ships and planes mercilessly pounded thousands of defeated Iraqi troops with virtually no defense; riddling the roadways with destroyed vehicles of troops and evacuees, forcing people into poverty and disease. That ties in with the second line, using *sea* to represent the Gulf.

The third line is vague. Many mothers were overwhelmed to see their sons return, but who merits this attention? It may describe the general circumstances. The last line is intriguing, in that *poison and letters hidden* could describe the mixed messages and secret communications between senior US officials and Saddam Hussein. Bush had headed the CIA. The Iraqi leader had been trained by the agency and enjoyed strong ties with it when the USA backed his war against Iran. Bush's diplomats had indicated to Hussein that it would not intervene if Iraq took action against Kuwait for drilling into Iraqi oil fields. That misunderstanding — or trick, as implied here — emboldened Iraq to invade its neighboring kingdom, thereby bringing destruction to its own land. The last line also connotes the mailing of anthrax virus after the attack on New York.

A nice fit, but line three remains unclear.

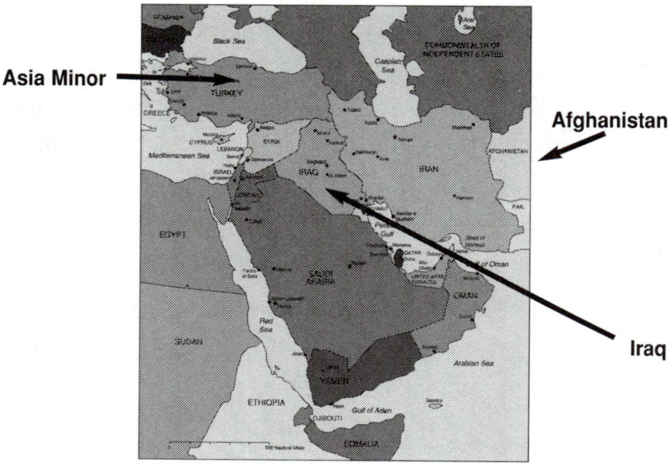

III:60

Par toute Asie grande proscription,
Mesme en Mysie, Lysie, & Pamphylie:
*Sang versera par absolution,**
D'un jeune noir remply de felonnie.

Throughout Asia there will be great proscription,
The same in Crete & Asia Minor:
Blood will flow because of the absolution*
Of a young dark man filled with criminality.

* Some transcriptions say *dissolution*, a word which means the same in French or English

WHO IS THIS GUY? — The first line certainly is an apt description of the rise of Islamic fundamentalism, with its Puritanism, intolerance, moralistic prohibitions and zealous punishments for free-thinking individuals. To that extent, it might also describe the international Drug War, although that is a more global *proscription* than he describes. The Taliban are located in Afghanistan, although fundamentalism has worked its way through both Africa and Asia, including the Phillipines.

The ancient geographic regions Nostradamus described in line two includes certain Muslim areas of the world today, but not Afghanistan and Iraq. Fundamentalists have a foothold in Turkey but not yet on the Mediterranean Island of Crete. Osama bin Laden's network, al Qaeda, has operatives in that area, but his forces are concentrated elsewhere.

Line three fits at least partially, in that blood has flowed due to wars and terrorism, but the last word presents a particular problem because of variances in the transcriptions we analyzed. Did Nostradamus mean *absolution*, the religious blessing of forgiveness (as in elevating murderers into martyrs), or did he mean *dissolution*, debauchery and secular corruption? The words are nearly opposite, but one can be given absolution for dissolution. This confusion again lends itself to the interpretation that there is a blur of religious and political motives mixed together so thoroughly that they cannot be fully extricated.

The last line applies because the attack was *criminal* and terrorism is a crime against humanity. The hijackers were all men, and relatively young. Unfortunately there is no way to date this event, so its currency is in doubt. However, there has been no holy war comparable to the Crusades since the writing hand penned this verse, until now.

I get a funny feeling that the *young dark man* of this quatrain knows something about what really happened.

Chapter 4

Hints at who may have done what

By now we must admit that Nostradamus had a pretty good image of human nature and the way at least some things were likely to shape up in modern times.

He did predict the rise of a great nation in the West, and even that there would be an aerial attack on New York or its approximate equivalent.

Those facts being given, a new question arises. What did Nostradamus envision about the perpetrators of the attack. At least, what did he write down that most closely resembles scenarios from the ongoing investigation? He did provide some possible clues, but not many specifics on dates, so you have to project from the context he provides.

As you continue, dear reader, please bear in mind that these are merely the poetic musings of an eccentric man from long ago. He was subject to the bias of his day, as we are to ours, so don't let that bias seduce you. He wrote many of his verses in such general terms that they can apply to a variety of situations, so his apparent accuracy may be more of a tribute to his craftiness than to any psychic, paranormal powers of prophesy. Remember that these verses are not facts or proof of anything, just images and analogies that can be attached to historical or current events.

Nostradamus himself gave warning about reading too deeply into his words, as posed in the introduction and at the end of this book (VI:100).

Please consider his advice.

VI:78

Crier victoire du grand Selin croissant,
Par les Romains sera l'Aigle clame,
Ticcin, Milan & Gennes ny consent,
Puis par eux mesmes Basil grand reclame.*

To shout the victory of Selin's great crescent,
Through the Romans
the Eagle will be proclaimed,
Pavia, Milan & Genoa do not consent,
Then through themselves the great Basil is
reclaimed.

* *Basil the Macedonian*, a Byzantine ruler who murdered the emperor and seized power in 867 AD

THE EAGLE & THE CRESCENT — The crescent moon banner was carried by *Selim the Grim*, a Turkish conqueror who lived in Nostradamus' day. It is a symbol of Islamic expansion, which in this case is juxtaposed with an Eagle.

The first line indicates a Muslim victory. The second line mentions the *Eagle*, a modern symbol of the USA. That implies a battle between a Muslim or Arabic state and the USA. (However, it must be noted that he used the eagle elsewhere to represent other historical entities, interpreted as Napoleon, the Holy Roman Empire, etc.)

If the Eagle is interpreted as America, then the *Romans* of line two may imply NATO, the modern, unified alliance that includes much of ancient Rome's European empire. After the slaughter in New York, NATO proclaimed the attack as being against the entire civilized world, and joined in the planned retaliation. Meanwhile, the deposed king of Afghanistan lives in Italy and did not *consent* to the rise of the Taliban. He condemned the terrorists and proposed to return to the throne to *reclaim* his homeland.

The last line paints the provocative image of a mystery person, characterized as *Basil*, a Ninth Century Byzantine usurper who murdered his emperor and seized the throne. It is not clear whether the group in the last line referred to as *themselves* are friends or foes of the Eagle. President Bush claimed that the main suspect in the New York attack, bin Laden, is "Wanted: Dead or Alive" by the USA. Alternatively, the Afghan people may themselves throw off the Taliban as pretenders to the throne, in the name of self determination. But will they reinstall the old king?

Nostradamus packed a lot of information into a few words here, with important historical allusions that may be even richer than they initially appear. Muslim expansion, Italian and American involvement, the return of a king, the capture of a usurper: It's an intriguing combination.

II:79

*La barbe crespe & noire par engin,**
Subjuguera la gent cruelle & fiere:
Le grand Chyren ostera du longin,
Tous les captifs par Seline baniere.

The beard frizzy & black by machine,
Will subdue the people cruel & proud:
The great Chiren will take from the tether,
All the captives through Selim's banner.

* *Engine* or *machine*, but also a *trap* or *skillful device*

THE MAN WITH THE BEARD — Osama bin Laden does resemble the character in line one. His *beard* is getting gray but still seems *black* enough, and *frizzy*. Bear in mind that under the Taliban's rule, men are not allowed to shave. They all have beards; as do many patriotic Americans.

Nostradamus didn't give a nationality for the person in line one, just the reference to Selim's crescent moon banner in line four. An airliner is a machine, so he describes the attack to that extent. His use of the word *engin* is taken as literal, but it also implies a *trap* or a *skillful tool*, which seems to recognize the evil brilliance required to pull off the simultaneous attacks on New York and Washington DC.

Despite great strength and deserved *pride*, US foreign policy has long been *cruel*. It slaughtered Indians, invaded Canada and Mexico, and instigated war with Spain. It now enforces painful economic blockades in Iraq and Cuba that cause great hardship for civilian populations. It lobs missiles deep into the homelands of its enemies with self-righteous arrogance. The USA's domestic policies of zero tolerance and the Drug War also hurts hundreds of thousands of its own citizens. Politicians are so afraid of being labeled "soft" in the media that they constantly pass penalties that are even more cruel. The word *subdued* works, not as conquered, but the nation had a period after the attack when people felt subdued, somber — even stunned. There were no planes in the air for a few days. It got quiet for a while.

The name *Chiren* in line three is Nostradamus' made-up name often thought to be an anagram. At times it has been interpreted as the name *Henric*; maybe you can figure it out. In essence, someone will free or take back lands or peoples that had been captured by someone whose banner has a crescent moon. The flags of Turkmenistan, Uzbekistan, Turkey and Pakistan do. Afghanistan, Iran and Iraq do not. After the attack, the USA again began funneling money to the Afghan resistance to Taliban rule.

II:9

Neuf ans le regne le maigre en paix tiendra,
Puis il cherra en soif si sanguinaire
Pour luy grand peuple sans foy & loy mourra,
Tué par un beaucoup plus debonnaire.

Nine years the reign
the thin man in peace will hold,
Then he will fall into a thirst so bloody
For him a great people
without faith & law will die,
Killed through a much better natured man.

REVENGE LONG PLOTTED — Osama bin Laden is the most conspicuously *thin man* to emerge as an identifiable icon of the attack on New York. Saddam Hussein has never looked very thin, but this may change. He and bin Laden are known to be enemies; but did they work together?

Otherwise, Hussein fits this verse better than bin Laden, who is implicated in many recent violent acts, such as the first World Trade Center bombing, February 26, 1993. For Hussein's part, *nine years ... in peace* elapsed from the Gulf War to 2000. The attack on New York in year ten meets this timeline. The word *thin* serves as a metaphor for the hunger caused by a decade of US government-applied economic, political and military sanctions on the people of Iraq. Air traffic is frozen there by a US-imposed "no fly zone." Iraq's military elite were humiliated, the royal palace bombed. Is a possible motive for the attack on New York in retaliation for the 1991 Gulf War and bombing of Bhagdad?

The second line describes an outburst of brutal violence. Certainly the term *bloodthirsty* applies to anyone who would mastermind the killing of 5000 people in the USA in one day. This would work pretty well, if Saddam loses a little weight, and if he had anything to do with it.

Which great people does Nostradamus refer to in line three? The USA has no state religion, so is it without faith? If it is taken for Iraq, it better explains the line. Many thousands of its people have died for Hussein; but Iraq was a secular state under him, not a theocracy. Fundamentalist clerics criticized his administration for, among other things, allowing women education and personal liberties. They rejected his 1991 call for a *jihad,* or holy war, to support his cause against the USA. Hussein faces charges of war crimes under international law; is he *without faith and law*?

And if those interpretations are used, who is the good-natured man mentioned at the end of the verse? We may not know until Hussein and bin Laden pass on.

VIII:20

Le faux message par election fainte
Courir par urben rompue pache arreste,
Voix aceptées, de sang chapelle tainte,
Et à un autre l'empire contraincte.

The false message through a rigged election
To run through the city stopping a broken pact,
Voices bought, chapel stained with blood,
And to another the empire is contracted.

RIGGED ELECTION, BROKEN TREATY — This verse has scattered elements that seem pertinent. GW Bush was put into office after a strongly disputed election.

His major opponent, Democrat Al Gore, won more popular votes nationally. Reports of the vote and ballot recounts for Florida — and therefore the Electoral College and the presidency — remain contradictory and contested. Some were right and others wrong, hence a *false message*. Ultimately the Supreme Court, not the voters, put Bush in office. Pundits labeled him a "selected" President, not elected. Some called it a *rigged election*, because all the judges who voted for GW Bush were politically or financially connected to his family. That could be characterized as having their *voices bought*, as in line three. Line two reminds one of the broken ABM treaty, the refusal to sign the international ban on germ and biological warfare, the pullout from the Kyoto global warming *pact*, or any of the other international pacts, agreements and treaties that Bush *broke* after taking office.

The *chapel stained with blood* in line three is difficult. Is it a metaphor of the World Trade Center towers as a temple to capitalism? Is it a literal image of a religious war, the death of church leaders, or people slain for their faith?

The last line is little help. If *the empire* of line four is taken as the USA, the phrasing could reflect the use of mercenaries in a military campaign. It could be military aid monies spent to persuade allies in the Gulf War or after the attack on New York. Egypt receives a huge amount of foreign aid. The USA forgave Pakistan billions in foreign debt to allow the staging of a military attack on Afghanistan, which led to large Muslim protests within Arab nations. With all the back room deals going on, it is unlikely we will ever know the long list of manipulations, agreements, *contracts* and payments that come into play during the course of events.

This intriguing verse is subject to broad interpretation.

Chapter 5

Beginning of the end?

At the time of this writing, the events of September 11, 2001 are still reverberating and its consequences are just beginning to unfold. Although there is no way to know which, if any, of these scenarios described by Nostradamus will occur, it is at least a curiosity to consider some of the unfulfilled predictions that may yet be realized.

We do not offer these as any certain future, but only in the sense that as events unfold we may recognize more of them in the words of this wily old prognosticator. Like any oracle, his words do not denote that which will be, but only what might yet become. We still have the ability to change the future. These verses are worth considering, if only to open our minds up to the possibilities that surround us.

If you follow the sense of the previous quatrains, you will see that Nostradamus felt that someone at the turn of the century would orchestrate a clever plot to bring down a mighty empire. It would involve an aerial attack on a major city, and certain parties would try to disguise it as a holy war, *jihad*, or perhaps even to trigger *Armageddon*, the war at the end of the world. However, Nostradamus hints that the whole plot would be a trap designed to draw an Empire into a final war, wherein it would sustain major casualties and stand to make only questionable gains.

The following is but a sampling of what he warns us to expect, if we take the bait and plunge into a global war, rather than treating the attack as an outrageous crime committed by a small group of conspirators. Like a slippery slope, he warns that every act has dangerous consequences.

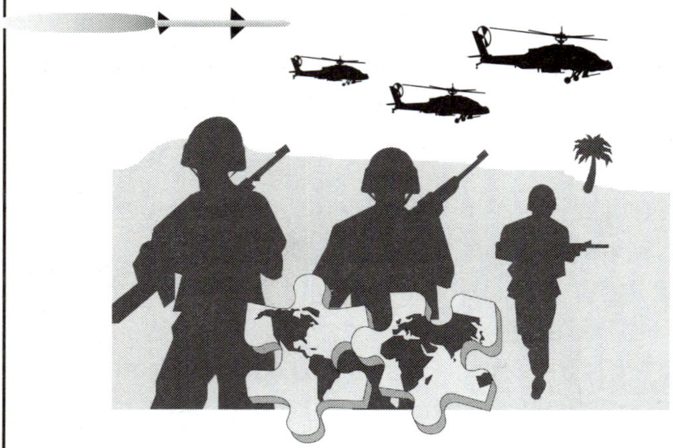

II:22

Le camp Ascop, d'Europe partira,*
S'adioignant proche de l'isle submergee:
D'Arton‡ classe phalange pliera,
Nombril du monde plus grand voix subroge.∞

The aimless army, from Europe will depart,
And join up close to the submerged island:
The Arton rank its standard folds,
The navel of the world substitutes
for a greater voice.

* Greek *askopos,* means *aimless*

‡ Greek *artos* means *bread;* considered an anagram for NATO

∞ From the Latin *subrogatus,* meaning *substitute*

AN ARMY ADRIFT — This verse took on new significance when the US Congress declared war on somebody who had not yet been identified for the attack on New York.

The first line refers to an *aimless army*, apparently one without a clear enemy, military objective, or limited timeline for its campaign. Perhaps it is aimed at the altogether wrong target. This force leaves from Europe, which is a staging area for the US forces, and also where NATO member nations have offered to undertake or support military action. Given the uncertainty of the task ahead or the identity of the actual perpetrators of the attack, this reference is dangerously close to the current situation.

There are several *submerged* ruins, as mentioned in line two, off the Mediterranean coast around Greece, Cyprus, Turkey and Asia Minor. After the attacks on New York and Washington, US ships were sent to the North Arabian Sea to shell Taliban-controlled regions of Afghanistan. The authors know of no submerged islands in that area.

Other interpreters have inferred the name *Arton* in line three as a Nostradamus anagram for NATO. *Folding up its standard* may be a metaphor for NATO setting aside its role as defender of Europe and expanding into a new role as defender of the civilized world. To that extent NATO forces also could be seen in line four to *substitute for a greater voice*, by supporting the superior military force of the USA. The *navel of the world* could reflect Europe's and the Mediterranean Sea's central geographical location in the world map, or the Middle East as the birthplace of civilization.

In sum, this seems to warn us against taking military action before the goals, targets, repercussions and deadlines are clear. It also indicates that the balance of power will at some point shift away from America back to Europe.

The whore of Babylon on her seven headed beast, that makes war with the Lamb, whom the Lamb shall overcome.

— Book of Apocalypse, Revelation Chapter 17, *The Bible*

I:55

Soubz l'opposite climat Babylonique,
Grande sera de sang effusion,
Que terre & mer, air, Ciel sera inique,
Sectes, faim, regnes, pestes, confusion.

In a land with the opposite climate to Babylon,
There will be of blood a great shedding,
That land & sea, air, Heaven will seem unjust,
Sects, hunger, kingdoms, plagues, confusion.

WORLD WAR III — Nostradamus makes a general allusion to a holy war that seems to occur in modern times, because of his reference in the third line to activities in the air.

The verse holds a geographic hint. *Babylon* was an ancient city in the area of Mesopotamia (Iraq) with a warm, arid *climate*. Any cool humid area could be *opposite*, like New York or farther north: Russia, Canada, the Arctic or Antarctic. Iraq and Afghanistan are both located within the band between 29 to 38 degrees North latitude. Curiously, some people today refer to New York City itself as Babylon. We leave any relevance in that to the reader's imagination.

The second line mentions a *great shedding of blood*, as occurs in any war. During the attack on New York, some 5,000 people died in about an hour. Line three mentions *heaven*, but Nostradamus' verb, *will seem*, again casts doubt on whether this is a religious crusade or simply a disguise for political war. If the Taliban invoke Allah while Christians declare "God's on our side," somebody is bound to be a bit disappointed and think *heaven seems unjust*. If the hijackers expected to go to heaven as martyrs for that attack, we think they were probably disappointed.

Nostradamus' line three phrase, *land and sea, air*, reminds us of the US Marine Corps song, "we will fight our country's battles on the land and air and sea." His final line connects religious *sects* and *kingdoms* to the terrible consequences of war: *hunger, plagues*, and *confusion*.

Talk about confusion! Who is the enemy? Where will they strike next? How do we defend against germ warfare?

This quatrain is frightening because of the scope of destruction implied. On the other hand, it is far too general to pinpoint. While holy wars have long been fought in the Middle East, what links this verse most closely to the modern situation is that this is the reference to the distinct climate zones.

Medieval Crusade scene.

IV:43

Seront ouys au Ciel les armes battre,
Celuy an mesme les divins ennemis:
Voudront loix sainctes injustement debatre,
Par foudre & guerre bien croyants à mort mis.

There will be heard in the Skies
weapons fighting,
The same year the divine are enemies:
They will want the holy laws to unjustly contest,
Through thunderbolt & war
many believers put to death.

AIR BATTLES & HOLY WARS — It could get pretty bad if the USA pursues warfare without finding a way to end the bloodshed. Bin Laden has already called it holy war. Middle Eastern grudges last for generations, so it will be protracted and based on "an eye for an eye" revenge.

The references that Nostradamus makes to a modern holy war and divine enemies were noted earlier, and they are horrible. Consider the Crusades, which lasted for centuries during the Middle Ages and destroyed many of Europe's most prominent leaders, who marched into the quagmire of war and disease, never to return. The air battle described in the first line, however, puts this quatrain squarely in modern times. In fact, it accurately describes the air campaign that opened up the Bush administration's first attack on Afghanistan on October 7, 2001. To his credit, Bush dropped food to the refugees of the war and has maintained that this is a war in terrorism, not a holy war. The US Constitution establishes separation of church and state.

Line two gives us an event occurring *the same year* as an air attack. The *divine enemies* would appear to be Islam and Christianity. The *unjust contest* mentioned in line three could be attached to all the innocent deaths in America, deaths of innocent Afghan civilians in the counterattack, or the invocation of Jesus' or Muhammad's names to rationalize indiscriminate killing. Jesus told his followers to love their enemy and turn the other cheek (Luke 6:27-29). "Blessed are the Peacemakers, for they shall be called the children of God. Blessed are those persecuted for righteousness' sake: For theirs is the kingdom of heaven." (Matthew 5:9) Many Muslims also distance themselves from violence.

The use of the phrase *thunderbolt and war* as weapons used to put many *believers* to death also sounds modern. *Thunderbolt* brings to mind missiles and long range missiles. Which believers are to die? It is not clear.

Illustration of the Apocalypse and the battle of Armageddon
— Book of Apocalypse, Revelations Chapter 17, *The Bible*

VIII:77

L'antechrist trois bien tost annichilez,
Vingt & sept ans sang durera sa guerre:
Les heretiques morts, captifs exilez,
Son corps humain eau rougie, gresler terre.

The antichrist very soon annihilates the three,
Twenty-seven years will last his bloody war:
The heretics dead, captives exiled,
Their human bodies red water, to hail down on the earth.

THE LONG WAR: ARMAGEDDON — It just gets worse. If our leaders plunge us too deeply into war, Nostradamus warns us to be ready for a long one.

Line one describes *the three* being annihilated in a long war with religious overtones. Who is the *antichrist*? This figure is mentioned in the *Bible* (I John 2:18) ,"whereby we know it is the last times." Who are the three? How will they be annihilated? The answers are not clear. Nonetheless, there are more details which we can ultimately compare to circumstances as they unfold. His scenario is a dire one, with *27 years of bloody war* mentioned in line two.

Since both sides of the conflict are running on blind faith rather than compassion and reason, both see each other as being *heretics*. So, in effect, everyone who subscribes to the notion of this being a holy war is a heretic from the point of view of their enemy. To the Taliban and other Muslim fundamentalists, the people who died in the World Trade Center were mostly heretics. To Christian fundamentalists, the Muslims are heretics because they treat Jesus as a prophet, not as God incarnate. Hence the first part of this line works. The *captives* being exiled could describe the individuals who were seized and deported from the USA, or perhaps from Afghanistan, where eight missionaries were arrested shortly before the attack on New York. If any are *exiled*, it would fit this description.

The fourth line fits a grisly description of the carnage at the World Trade Center, where people jumped from the buildings, and blood and body parts rained down to earth, or *hailed* down, to use Nostradamus' more poetic phrase. But this does not read as a one-day event, this seems to be a terrible and protracted war.

It's okay with us if Nostradamus got all this stuff wrong. Still, it is up to the global community to decide if we fulfill these prophesies or chart a better course for humanity.

I:62

La grande perte las! que feront les lettres,
Avant le cicle de Latona parfaict,*
Feu, grand deluge, plus par ignares sceptres
Que de long siecle ne se verra refaict.

The great loss so tiresome!
that will become of the literature,
Before the cycle of the moon is completed,
Fire, great flood, by more ignorant rulers
How long the century
until it is seen restored.

* A mythological name for the moon

A NEW DARK AGE — This bleak verse seems to portray a future dark age that lasts a hundred years, accompanied with much human suffering. This is a common theme of science fiction, but fortunately has not yet occurred.

According to line one, a *great loss ... of literature* lies ahead. A lot of economic data and human knowledge were lost in the attack on New York, but our sense is that Nostradamus means something on an even more grand scale. There is no religious reference, so he seems to refer to secular knowledge, although it might describe a library, archive or other single body of scientific information.

According to line two, this may happen in a matter of less than a month, if the *cycle of the moon* is taken as being from full to full. That occurs every 28 days. On the other hand, the lunar calendar intersects with the solar calendar every 12 years, so this learning may erode more slowly.

This coincides with both *fire and flood* in line three, when ignorant persons hold power. There are always fires and floods; but while GW Bush admits he's no genius, his initial response to the attack was well thought out. News reports say bin Laden is not only low tech, but "no tech." The Taliban leaders, meanwhile, eschew western science and forbid women to be educated. The US political *leaders* who wanted to "bomb them back to the stone age" in revenge showed their own *ignorance*, because both Afghanistan and Iraq have already been pounded back to the stone age: Afghanistan by decades of civil war and war with Russia, and Iraq during and since the Gulf War.

Line four indicates a *long century* passing before human knowledge is *restored*. Hopefully the USA will allow these societies to re-emerge out of the Dark Age and into the light of science and technology sooner than that.

There is no dating device given to tell if this warning is meant for our lifetime or some later generation.

X:66

Le chef de Londres par regne l'Americh,
L'isle d'Escosse t'empiera par gelée:
Roy Rebauront un si faux Antechrist,*
Que les mettra trestous dans la meslée.

The chief of London
through the power of America,
The Isle of Scotland will be tempered by frost:
The King of the Rebels will have
a fraudulent antichrist,
Who will place them all into the conflicts.

* *Rebelle* means rebel, from which this appears to derive

AN AMERICAN ANTICHRIST — In case things were not bad enough, here comes Nostradamus' strongest warning to *America*. This is the only of his quatrains to mention by name America, which had only recently been "discovered."

Line one brings the United Kingdom into the picture; the *chief of London* would seem to be the Prime Minister of England — Tony Blair enthusiastically supported the military attacks on Afghanistan — or a member of the royal family. He is drawn into a situation through America. In line two, *Scotland* is made colder, whether by physical temperature or a chilling of the political climate.

By line three, things get interesting. *King Rebauront* could be the President of the USA. Nostradamus' use of "Reb" seems to indicate that this would be after the colonies had rebelled against England. (What's fascinating is that England did not yet have established colonies in America when Nostradamus died. Not only did he anticipate their creation, he also foresaw that they would rebel and become free, as described in quatrain VII:80, not included in this book). In this verse, the USA is tied to a an *antichrist*. This Biblical character is a false Christ figure who is linked to Armageddon, the final battle between good and evil prior to the second coming of Christ, the raising of the dead, etc. This battle is described in Revelation, chapter 19-20.

The last line seems to predict that an American ruler and his charlatan, pseudo-christian adviser will manage to bring the whole world *into the conflicts*. The formation of a global alliance has become a mainstay of US foreign policy. It is taking place again as we write this book. NATO forces and individual governments, have been enlisted into this cause.

Clearly today is a difficult time, when military, medical and other responses are needed to fight terrorism. The warning here seems not to be seduced by calls for a holy war — or we may face even more dire consequences as a result.

Chapter 6

Better things to come?

While it is easy to subscribe to the doom and gloom of Nostradamus' predictions that might relate to this terrible event, the Renaissance prognosticator also offers an alternative scenario for how these problems might be resolved.

One of the reasons his verses are so artful and well formulated is that they are nebulous enough to be fitted against many situations. He wrote vivid and detailed scenarios, and leaves it to us to find the correlations. What fits fits, and what doesn't doesn't. Other people may read these same quatrains given here and find connections to different events throughout history. Since his writings cover thousands of years, we dare not presume that these particular disasters are for our generation, if they prove true at all.

His quatrains give several alternative scenarios to choose from as we leave our mark on the history of the world. One vision he shared is an Armageddon-type war that crushes civilization, unleashes terrible plagues, famine and war, and degenerates into a new Dark Age.

Nostradamus also points toward a lighter path of good leadership and solutions, and it is up to us to decide which path to take and how to fulfill our own destiny. While no one doubts that America is rightfully aggrieved and angry at the September 11, 2001 attack, the response must be well thought out and the long term consequences considered.

The following verses speak of mercy, justice, peace and the rule of law. They are included here in the hope that our readers and the leaders on all sides of this tragedy will choose the path of reason and break the cycle of violence.

III:27

Prince Lybinique puissant en Occident,
François d'Arabe viendra tant enflammer:
Scavans aux lettres sera condescendent,
La langue Arabe en François translater.

A Libyan prince will be powerful in the West,
The French will be so enamored of the Arab:
Learned in literature he will condescend
To translate the Arab language into French.

AN ARAB ALLY — If applied to today, this verse indicates that an Arabic person has the special knowledge and communication skills needed to help resolve this crisis.

The first line says a *Libyan prince* will gain power in the West. Libyan leader Col. Muammar Gaddafi is not royalty, but he is closest to being such. In recent years, Libya has tried to mediate Muslim crises in Sudan, the Congo and the Phillipines. It paid damages to victims of the 1989 bombing of French flight UTA 772. It turned over two suspects in the 1988 bombing of Pan Am flight 103. Gaddafi condemned the September 11 attacks and has called on Muslims to fight terrorism. Since the USA is still suspicious of him and lists Libya as a sponsor of terrorism, an intermediary might be needed to bridge the gap between them and end terrorism.

In line two, *the French* are said to like *the Arab* and play a role in his efforts. Perhaps this applies to someone other than Gaddafi. The third line says this person is *learned in literature;* perhaps a well-educated diplomat or an academic, perhaps a scholar of the *Koran* who can challenge the hard line interpretation of the fundamentalists. The final line states that this Libyan helps *translate Arabic into French.* Since these languages have long been translated, might he translate a document that sheds light on this crisis? Is he an encryption expert who can crack the code of the terrorists or even help capture them? Can he help improve relations between Muslims and the West? Is he so influential that his personal communications can change the course of events?

While certainly not an endorsement of Gaddafi, this verse does remind us not to close ourselves off to anyone who may be of help. If America falls into stereotypes and scapegoating, it may reject the very people who can most help. If it abandons its core principles of human equality and personal liberty, the terrorists will have won.

Freedom, justice and diversity make the USA what it is. We need everyone to pull together, now more than ever.

V:41

Nay sous les umbres & journée nocturne,
Sera en regne & bonté souveraine,
Fera renaistre son sang de l'antique uerné,
Renouvellant siecle d'or pour l'airain.

Born beneath the shadows & a dark day,
He will in influence & kindness be sovereign,
He will revive his blood of the ancient urn,
Renewing the century of gold for the brass.

A JUST AND MERCIFUL LEADER — This verse offers the hope of a leader who will heal schisms and defuse crises rather than perpetuate violence.

If we take September 11, 2001 to be the *dark day* in line one, we have several ambiguities. Is this the actual birth date of a person, or simply the beginning of their journey to power? Are the *shadows* the gloom of smoke and dust in New York after the attack, placing this person physically in the city, or simply the dark consequences of that day that will affect him, wherever he may be? Could he be a Middle Eastern person who brings an era of tolerance to the Muslim world? Will he be empowered soon, or many years later, after growing to adulthood?

Line two presents a *kind* leader who gains *influence* as a result of being kind, not intolerant or punitive. Mercy is the basis of his political mandate. The third line is cryptic: What is this *ancient urn*? Does this leader *revive his blood* through marriage, ritual, or social power? What about elections?

The last line holds two possibilities. Either he will ring in a new golden age to replace one of brass, or he will replace a *century of gold*, i.e., wealth and greed, with *brass* — a more practical and fair system. The 20th century was, indeed, an era of innovation and wealth, but also of disparity and poverty. When Ronald Reagan assumed the office of President, he led the country into an era of social intolerance and conspicuous consumption. He inspired the "Me Generation" and glorified consumerism, personal wealth and luxury to the neglect and detriment of both society and the environment. Why did we not see this attack coming? Has American materialism blinded us to the anger and hatred that our exploitation stirred up around the world?

This verse brings us hope for a positive future in spite of, or even because of, the tragedy of September 11. At any rate, the attack should be heeded as a wake up call.

VI:24

Mars & le sceptre se trouvera conjoint,
Dessous Cancer calamiteuse guerre:
Un peu apres sera nouveau Riy oingt,
Qui par long temps pacifiera la terre.

Mars & the scepter will be in conjunction,
Under Cancer a calamitous war:
Shortly thereafter a new king will be anointed,
Who for a long time will bring peace to the earth.

A NEW LEADER BRINGS PEACE — If we use astronomical dating, and the scepter in line one implies Jupiter (the Roman king of the gods), the next time this rare planetary alignment will occur is on June 21, 2002, at the beginning of Cancer. If one instead interprets *Mars* (the god of war) to symbolize war, and *the scepter* as a symbol of political power, it connotes a warlike government.

Either way, line two seems to imply a short but *calamitous* war with devastating impact. If the entire war is fought under Cancer, that is just a month of fighting. Alternatively, it may begin then and continue longer.

Our interest is drawn to line three, which says that a new leader will *be anointed* into power. No nationality is given. If applied to the USA, this reference could mean a President who leads the global community into a long era of *peace*.

There will be no national elections in the USA between the attack and November 2002. Bush will be well into his term of office, so he won't exactly be a *new king*. Vice President Cheney hardly represents anything new, either, tied as he is to the Reagan and Bush Sr. administrations. That leaves the political primaries, which set the stage for the Senate and Congressional races. Maybe a Congressional or cabinet official will achieve new power. Maybe a new President will take office in 2004.

Getting this specific with a date is very gutsy of the old seer, because we can really evaluate his accuracy. We've seen him miss by years in other efforts. Perhaps this is meant for another conjunction than that in 2002. In any case, we hope that such a leader does emerge to usher in an age of peace.

That's about all for this verse; not much detail except for the given date. We might want to begin to seek out or cultivate new leaders who are capable of bringing peace instead of relying on war to prop up our standard of living.

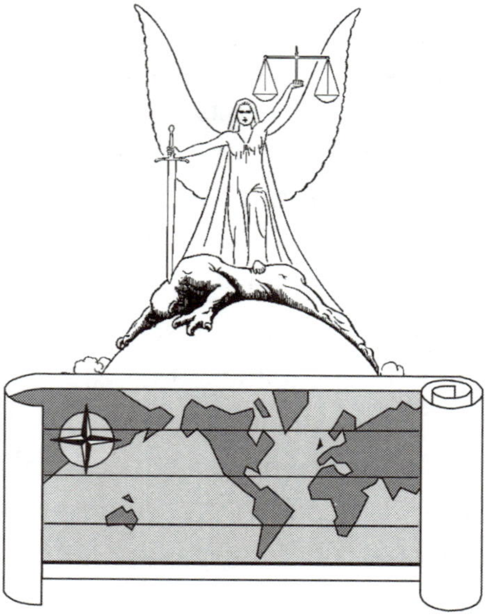

IX:66

Paix, union sera & changement,
Estats, Offices, bas hault, & hault bien bas,
Dresser voyage, le fruict premier torment,
Guerre cesser, civils proces, debats.

Peace, union there will be & change,
Estates, Offices, low high, & high very low,
To prepare for journey, the first fruit torment,
War to cease, civil process, debates.

THE RULE OF LAW — Here Nostradamus portrays an optimistic outcome: a well-ordered global society.

The first line is wonderful to read: *peace, union … change.* One thing that is clear is that a change is at hand, and we hope and pray it will be in the direction of peace. What union may be at hand? Ecumenism between the Muslim and Christian churches seems unlikely. A balance between the self-indulgent wastefulness of the USA's consumerism and the enforced austerity of fundamentalist Islam? Egalitarianism rather than a social chasm separating the haves from the have-nots? More tolerance and social acceptance at home and abroad? Some balance clearly needs to be struck.

Line two seems to describe justice and egalitarianism, noting that the highs and lows are shifting. *Estates* refers to hereditary wealth. *Offices* could be interpreted as business work spaces, but since it is capitalized in the original, we think Nostradamus refers to civil government. The tables then are turned between high and low; but in what sense? Political power? Military strength? Civil liberties? Riches?

Perhaps the *journey* of line three is literal, but again it seems more likely that Nostradamus used the poetic sense, as in the journey from war to peace. *First fruit* is a phrase that refers to the firstborn child, which does apply to GW Bush, among others. The nature of his *torment* could be physical or mental, as he comes to grips with his Christian conscience and the difficult decisions he is facing.

This is a profound task. The path Nostradamus points to is a journey toward peace and a better world. Societies must break the cycle of violence and revenge and replace *war* with Rule of Law, *civil* rights and social justice. The gap between rich and poor must be bridged. We must respect nature and the human rights of all. Finally, we need free speech to publicly *debate* every course of action, so we don't repeat history — or fulfill ancient prophesies of doom.

VI:100

LEGIS CAUTIO CONTRA INEPTOS CRITICOS

Qui legent hosce versus, maturé censunto:
Prophanum vulgus & inscium ne attrectato;
Omnesque Astrologi, Blenni, Barbari procul sunto,
Qui aliter faxit, is rité sacer esto.

WARNING AGAINST INEPT CRITICS

Those who read this verse
should think upon it maturely:
The profane, vulgar &
ignorant should not be attracted;
All astrologers,
idiots and barbarians stay away,
He who does otherwise,
let him be a priest to the rite.

A WARNING FROM THE MAN — In the verse on the facing page, Nostradamus himself warns against using his poems to foretell the future. It is easier — and safer — to recognize known events as corollaries than it is to accurately predict the years and centuries to come.

So please, dear reader, don't be hasty in making condemnations based on these cryptic words, he reprimands. If we misinterpret his words, that is not his fault. Their significance will unfold in due time.

In conclusion, we must again point out that this book was begun on September 12, 2001, the day after the attack on New York. It has been a month in the preparation, and so will be published in the midst of the events we seek to analyze for your consideration.

It is unavoidable that the unfolding of events will shed light on the circumstances of this world-changing day and that new information and incident will arise. To the extent that future knowledge or incident may supercede the connections we have developed, we beg your understanding.

This is why we have tried to exercise restraint in making any certain pronouncements about whether these were predictions being fulfilled, or simply the best guesses of an obviously very ingenious poet. We cannot tell you what Nostradamus saw, only what he wrote. The images and details to which we allude are the doings of individuals and society, not to be blamed on the writings of an old man.

Yet, we cannot help but wonder at his craft. This book only looks at one series of images from nearly a thousand, while uncounted others have been lost to time.

So we turn the page one more time, and close our book, for the time being at least.

Thank you for sharing it with us.

Index

Quatrains

I:1	10
I:2	10
I:35	9
I:41	54
I:50	40
I:55	72
I:62	78
I:63	46
I:87	24
I:91	52
II:9	64
II:19	38
II:22	70
II:29	14
II:30	23, 30
II:46	9, 20
II:79	62
II:89	50
III:27	84
III:60	56
IV:43	74
V:41	86
VI:34	16
VI:24	88
VI:78	60
VI:97	9, 18
VI:100	10, 59, 92
VII:80	76
VIII:20	66
VIII:70	48
VIII:77	76
IX:51	42
IX:65	44
IX:66	90
IX:73	34
IX:92	28
X:39	9
X:49	22
X:72	26
X:74	35
X:66	80

Alphabetic Listings

1 John 2:18	77
America	81
anthrax	21, 55
antichrist	77, 81
August 2010	34
Babylon	23, 49, 31, 73
beard	63
bin Laden	15, 57, 61, 63, 65
blue turban	34
Bush	17, 29, 55, 67, 79, 92
calendar	79
Christian	25, 43, 75, 77, 81, 92
dark age	79, 83
eagle	61
election	67
environment	39, 43, 49
free speech	92
golden age	88
holy war	25, 53, 57, 65, 73, 75, 77
Hussein	15, 49, 55, 65
Iraq	27, 41, 49, 55, 57, 63, 79
June 21, 2002	90
King Reb	81, 89
Luke 6:27-29	75
Matthew 5:9	75
millennium	35
Mongols	27
NATO	61, 71, 81
moon	45, 79
Nostradamus	9, 10
poison	55
peace	90, 92
president	41, 81, 90
Revelation	49, 72, 81
SDI / star wars	53, 67
terror	27, 31
thin man	65
transcriptions	11
treaties	53, 67
Washington DC	63

Your notes